Learning to Survive
INFINITY

Steven J. Bingel

authorHOUSE®

AuthorHouse™
1663 Liberty Drive
Bloomington, IN 47403
www.authorhouse.com
Phone: 1 (800) 839-8640

Published by AuthorHouse 08/12/2015

ISBN: 978-1-5049-2861-8 (sc)
ISBN: 978-1-5049-2860-1 (e)

CONTENTS

∞

When I first began this book I had so many ideas and things to say that I had a hard time staying focused on any *one* thing. Certainly any one chapter itself could easily be extrapolated and contain enough information for one book itself. So rather than making each chapter long and drawn out I have chosen to mix things around and sometimes reiterate important correlations and ideas so that the reader doesn't get lost in any one idea. After all, in order to understand how the world is and how we relate to it requires letting go of our usual focus and rather staying in touch with the *feel* of a given situation or concept that certainly cannot be put into words.

Please understand, I make no claims of being a physicist in the classical sense or of having even a fraction of all the information available today about quantum physics. It is just that many new discoveries are immediately translated and justified for lack of better words, into some theory. One must remember that no one theory or equation can ever contain all the information in the universe. Rather, we must focus on ourselves and how we relate to that information and how we can better our current world for the short time we are here to affect it.

My favorite metaphor that translates this best for me is Aleph (א) from the Kabalistic religion. It is a mythical point that contains all other points in space and time---a moment that contains all other moments. I believe all our experiences gathered in life somehow relate to the materialistic world around us and vice versa. At any given moment all the information available is contained both within the whole and as *part* of the whole. Just like a hologram, whose whole is contained in any one of the sum of it's parts, so is life. Life is synchronistic, as are our lives. In it's origin synchronicity is the creative moment from which the whole pattern of order in one's life can be perceived as it spreads out into the future. It will appear very natural to one's mind that it constantly sensitive to change, for it reveals the overall patterns of nature and mind and provides a context in which events have their meaning. There will be meaningful relationships between inner and outer events. It is these relationships which are the main focus of this book. We all already know more about the world than we realize, for after all, every human mind contains the sum of all knowledge since the beginning of time. However, unlocking those secrets and bringing them to the surface is the basis for the drive of life. It is what keeps us full of passion and pushes us to succeed.

Counterfactuals allow us to test whether something might have happened, but didn't. And quantum physics allows real effects to result from counterfactuals. There will be higher than average occurrences of events as in probability theory, but a large ensemble of probabilistic events will always average out where individual happenings and events can be ignored. Any one event is in-deterministic. It acts to hide the effects of individual fluctuations within the overall average, however it remains there, hidden, all the same….waiting for us to discover it.

I have wanted to write this book since I was a kid. Perhaps I didn't possess the faculties to do so until this latter point in my life. I would rather think that the verbiage just wouldn't be as ornate. As you shall read, I probably was better off *not* knowing what I now do, as it has only clouded my childish point of view.

CHAPTER 1

Why Grass Can't Be Red

Today I was speaking to a second grade class about birds. We were discussing their biology, habits, song and morphology. Some children were very receptive and asked many questions. Most, as often happens at such a young age, were preoccupied with other endeavors, such as the person sitting next to them, or a spider climbing on the ceiling. For those who had the least interest I went to great pains to insure that they understood I was by no means an *expert* in this particular field of ornithology, but rather an observer like themselves.

Schools often tend to compile students into neat little learning packages as if they were software with the teacher or guest speakers' words becoming the program written on their brains. Little or no room is left for creative thinking, thinking "outside-the-box" so to speak. As we progressed with the talk, which remained wholly interactive throughout, the children who were really in-tune with what I was saying started realizing patterns and correlations, then formulated hypotheses on their own. They were "getting" my underlying message, not just as it pertains to bird biology, but to each and every bit of information that could be put forth to challenge their conceptual learning abilities, that they weren't limited to something that was told to them by an *expert*, but each had his or her ability to formulate strategies and methods of uncovering information on their own. This was by far, one of the few times where I felt connected to my subject and to my listeners, and if I had to guess, I would say each felt connected to me. We were embraced in an oscillation of information exchange.

This has not been the first such time that I had felt this connectedness. However, not all interaction carries the same amount of connectedness, some none at all. In my present occupation I have experienced many such opportunities. Some I have taken great pleasure in pursuing and have found myself in wonderful conversations. Others have fallen flat. The ones that touch me the most I recall even today, although some took place many years ago. How can this be? How is it that the human brain retains the capacity to meld all experiences into coherent and everlasting stories? Upon what "medium" do these conversations, experiences and thoughts get written? Is there some biological existence to memory? Can we point to one particular part of the brain and say that this is where memory lives or is stored?

These and many more are questions that have stricken mankind for centuries. Since my childhood I have always had an interest in science and biology. It all culminated with pursuit of a degree in wildlife management and the associated courses that really ignited the fire within to seek out answers to all these questions I mentioned in the paragraph before. A tall order by any means for anyone to accomplish, but I figure I have all my life to "experience" and "correlate" and see patterns and relationships.

Like my second grade students mentioned before, I have tried to maintain an attitude of "ancient wisdom" for my fifty-three years of experience-gathering. What I mean by this, is that like all good science, anything that has already been put forth by another scientist within his or her respective field, and done according to accepted methods, is taken and built upon by all future science within it's particular discipline. I accept, sometimes at face value, all work that has been done before me to be sound and true, and seek to expand upon that which is known to that which I would like to know. The only exception is that my attitude of "ancient wisdom" allows me license to think outside traditional or even accepted methods if I can create a dialogue within my framework of science where others may experience my experiences, think my thoughts and speak my language.

But is this wholly possible? Can we actually somehow "align" ourselves with others so that they may speak our language, think our thoughts and experience our experiences? Do we as living, breathing, thought-processing, biological, flesh-and-blood entities possess faculties both physical and metaphysical that may allow us to transcend an either physical or metaphysical believing world. In other words, does the capacity within our-self exist to see beyond ourselves and outside ourselves to extend these experiences and thoughts and language from within ourselves to within another?

Present day science in quantum physics has found startling similarities in human psychology and consciousness to how the microscopic world works. Terms like particle/wave duality being paired with words like both/and rather than traditional Newtonian physics which used pairings such as either/or. What all this means is that things in the realm of the real small (we're talking atomic sized) aren't always as they seem. Particles which are small bits of matter behave as if they are everywhere at once and the mere act of looking at them fixes their position both in time and space and assumes there to be waves along with particles. The waves behave as their name implies, rather than being a singular point or bit, they appear as curved lines, much as the letter C does in this sentence. Both particles and waves have the ability to interact (theoretically) with each other. Sometimes in coherent oscillations which result in all particles and waves behaving in the same manner. This has been shown to be the case with things like laser beams in-which all individual photons of light are "in-tune" with one another. Whereas light normally scatters as soon as it leaves the source, coherent laser light, because each of it's individual photons are oscillating in unison with one another, is concentrated and therefore continues in a straight line configuration for a long ways depending on the power input and frequency being used.

These oscillations in unison are referred to as Bose-Einstein condensates, named after the two people who were instrumental in discovering them. Bose-Einstein condensates or BEC's as they are often called, are being studied for their possible application in the computer industry because of their usefulness in processing information at fast speeds. Research has been slow because achieving coherent oscillations in unison in any of our man-made materials requires very cold temperatures.

BEC's also happen in not-so-cold temperatures and in all of the unlikely places, the human brain. Research has shown that apical dendrites exist on the cerebral cortex which when stimulated correctly will oscillate in unison at precisely the correct frequency to achieve a BEC like state. This produces the background upon which consciousness can master it's art. It is even believed that these oscillations can be extended outside their biological boundaries and interact with the BEC's that are occurring within individuals mutually involved in conversation, learning or other similar endeavors.

So, with that all said, is it possible to extend our thinking and say that "oscillating dendrites" contain our experience, our language and our thoughts?---probably not, only because our bodies are constantly in a process of renewal. Unfortunately, even though flesh and blood systems are extremely resilient and can achieve phenomenal things, cells and living tissue require updating every so often. Every atom will be totally exchanged at least once within a period of seven years. So how could living, biological entities like brains ever retain memory and experience? Now you know where the expression "hold that thought" comes from. Is it possible that through evolutionary processes that information gets written on DNA itself? Dare we think such thoughts? Could this actually happen?

So, to get back to the central theme of this chapter, why isn't grass red? It isn't that it couldn't be red or any other color for that matter. What color it is, is dependent upon the level of reality in which it is being interpreted. Reality by quantum definitions is one emergent possibility plucked out of a sea of many possibilities. It is a collapsing of our quantum wave function into one singularity. Whereas grass could be any one of many colors, human eye structure dictates perceived color at a level of mutually agreed upon perception of color by all that have perceived grass as "green" in the past.

It really consists of a multi-faceted process which we shall delve into even further. First, is the fact that many possibilities (colors) exist that the grass may become, any of which may be picked dependent upon collapsing the quantum wave function by observing it. Secondly, our eye structure has evolved as such that all human eyes perceive things that are associated with the photon wavelength that mutually agrees with stored information in our brains as green to be green. And lastly, someone at some point in time had given a name to the perceived color associated with things like grass as green.

If you were the first person ever to see grass, how would you describe it? How *could* you describe it without other experiences or related events upon which to draw? Language and description is a whole series of hierarchical ambiguities, many possibilities until one is plucked out and applied. Why can't people who have claimed to have had extra-terrestrial experiences (close encounters of the third kind), describe what they saw, heard or felt? Could it possibly be at the same level of an individual encountering grass or any new experience for the first time...that is to say that they have no other experiences or similar information as of yet processed upon which to draw on?

So, grass *can* be red, green or any color for that matter. What it *is* is dependent upon the circumstances upon which it finds itself in. In the case of human beings collapsing the quantum wave function by the mere act of observation and solidifying only one possibility for the eye to relate back to the brain and intermingle with mutually exclusive correlations of experience, we *see* green. Hence, grass isn't red, can't be red within the situation within which it finds itself as observed by humans.

It is said that when Columbus and his crew first visited the New World that the inhabitants he encountered living there had no knowledge of the outside world and could not see the boats on the horizon as they approached the shore. How could this be? Only their Shaman had the insight to see something that the others were missing. He looked and looked and eventually he saw ripples on the surface of the water and eventually the ships. This knowledge he passed on to the rest and soon they all could see the ships. It took one person with an open mind and the ability to think outside the accepted realm of thinking to believe that something was there and his experience as translated to the others made it real.

CHAPTER 2

Biology at Work

How does all this happen? What physical processes must be happening? Where do they happen? Human eyes are composed of rods and cones and the inner lining of the eye receives images and all associated physical information. It is then sent to the brain via the optic nerve. Chemical reactions then take over the processing of information as it gets relayed from one neural synapse to the next. Electrical charges are generated by ionic channels within cell walls as they open and close during this chemical information process. It is these small electrical charges which induce a BEC within all associated neurons which acts as a kind of superconductor and the whole process is sped up. This continues on through to the brain where anything perceived as associated with the information being received also starts to oscillate in unison, that is, all stored information available pertinent to *this individual experience,* unless it is being perceived for the first time whereas no oscillating can happen. The quantum wave function collapses at this point and selects (like evolution) the individual event and transcribes it to DNA. That is to say that a new event, bit of information or experience is literally collapsed into fixed reality when no background BEC is available against which to *compare notes with.* New experiences and bits of information have to be written into genetic code or else they would be lost when all of our atoms get replaced once every seven years.

Similar evolutionary processes take place in plants. Some of which at the cellular level resemble those processes we just described in the simple act of observing something new for the first time or having an original thought or experiencing some fresh idea.

For example, in the metabolic pathways of glycolysis, growth hormones are produced, chiefly auxins, cytokinins and gibberellins. Which are produced and in what amount seems to stem from the circumstances in which the plant finds itself---sound familiar? For example, plant biology research has shown that certain red mulches when applied underneath tomato plants improve fruit yield. This has even been extended to below-ground development. It appears that the frequency of light reflected back from red mulch stimulates plant growth hormones to be produced in greater than otherwise normal amounts found in other color stimulus. Why would or could this be? Why far-red light? Why not ultra-violet light which packs more energy into a shorter photon length? Perhaps 400 million years ago when the earth was younger and spinning faster than it does today plants *did* use ultra-violet light. Days were shorter and plants that were biologically capable of using ultra-violet light would be selected over plants that could not. Perhaps the gene for fast growth (use of ultra-violet light) was beneficial then, but now where days are longer because the earth is spinning slower, no advantage is gained by plants that have recessive genes for using ultra-violet light. However, plants that can utilize far-red light do have an advantage. Those recessive genes are still present because DNA was written upon at the level of BEC oscillations---collapsing as the amount of available light was short---and again written upon as the earth began to spin slower and available light increased.

Recent research in quantum gravity also seems to indicate that things have evolved since the time when dinosaurs roamed the earth. Although it seems that the laws that govern all physics have been present since the *beginning,* gravity may have had less of an effect on the dinosaurs, hence the largeness of their size would seem to have been dictated by the necessity of staying put and not floating around. But, to say that gravity is a thing would be wrong of us, rather it is a state which exists as a secondary byproduct of the existence of any particular object, be it a planet, human or dinosaur and the distortion the object exerts on space-time. Gravity is the final, fixed state in which an object exists after it's many possibilities are explored. The time that transpires between the existence of it's many possibilities and it's final state is determined by the mass of the object. The smaller it's mass, the larger the amount of time that it exists in multiple states. The larger it's mass, the shorter the amount of time. As an object approaches the speed of light, the larger it's mass becomes until it reaches infinity. This is why it is possible only for mass-less objects like photons and hadrons to achieve the speed of light, and why larger physical objects are always here and now and things on a quantum level are capable of being in many places at the same time. Gravity is nothing more than the lowest energy state upon which an object ends up. The energy required to maintain a particular state becomes greater and greater until a lower energy state is achieved.

One other similarity in science *jumps out* at me. Covalent bonds occur between substances in which electrons are shared. These substances combine to form other substances. Electrons are often referred to as discreet energy packets separate from other quanta such as photons. In the spirit of quantum thinking let's assume that *both* electrons *and* photons are one in the same. How they manifest themselves depends upon the situation in which they find themselves. They are *both* electrons *and* photons during transitions in a BEC state of intermingling, smearing themselves out everywhere at once and taking quantum leaps from one energy state to another, overlapping waves with all probabilities before them. Since they are photons traveling at the speed of light until at some point they are observed and their wave function is collapsed and they present themselves as electrons. Thus, they would only be capable of traveling at a predetermined speed half that of the speed of light.

Why is it that when listening to a particular piece of music or reading a book that our mind's eye will see what it is that we hear or are reading? How does this happen? What if we have no experience to correlate what we are hearing or have read? Why do I see one thing while you another? For instance, if I ask you to picture a high mountain pasture in your mind, what do you see? Perhaps a scene from the movie "Heidi" or something from a TV commercial...I know what I see. I have been to Alaska. It was here that I hunted Dall sheep and my experience allows me to picture a specific place in my mind's eye. A place that struck me as beautiful, the most strikingly beautiful place I have yet visited. It stands as the epitome of a high mountain pasture and all things associated with any particular thought of high mountain pastures automatically brings this singular experience to the surface of my consciousness. There are distinct textures, hues of color and even sounds and smells that will elicit this very memory. It is a complete experience not lacking in any aspect of the *actual* experience and bringing it to mind's eye is like experiencing it for the first time all over again. It causes the same feelings to stir inside me that were associated with my original experience. Both the original experience and the memory elicited by some trace element of it are in actuality one in the same.

If one looks into a mirror and sees a reflection of oneself, which is the original and which is the "copy"? Who is to say that the mirror does not merely reflect the original image but *is* the original and the original is but a mere copy of the reflection?

Who is the wiser man...one who can manipulate numbers into a language (that only he and a handful of others may understand) to explain why things are so, and to what end or means, for his own comfort or to benefit all?...or the man with his own hands and limited knowledge and a few simple tools who may create great works of art-from cabinetry-to houses-to finely crafted cuckoo clocks with intricate detail, paintings, complete symphonies or even cities? Has not either man accomplished the greater of things? For themselves and their fellow men? Of course, one without the other and neither would need to exist right? Does both require the use of mind? Which "thinks" more? One more completely than the other? In different context? Do different cultures employ the same methods in thinking? For example, do the Chinese think in Chinese? Or in some common symbolical form of thought?

Does not the creation of great works of art require similar skills as those employed by the mathematician? And vice versa...in discovering new methods of solving difficult problems, must not the mathematician use creative skills to create and solve equations that will fit a particular circumstance? Can it then be said that both must create and use similar tools and skills in their pursuits?

Which is more important in the makeup of a fine wooden cabinet? The cabinet can be comprised of any wood-pine, cherry, ash, oak, mahogany or teak. Is it the wood that is most important? Without nails, screws and glue the wood could not be compiled into a cabinet. Are the nails, screws and glue the most important constituents of the cabinet? Without the wood they would be just nails, screws and glue-nothing more. What about the fine crystal glass that adorns the door and allows inspection of the cabinet's contents. Is it the most important? It does give rigidity and keeps out dust and allows light through so one can see inside. But without the wood and nails and glue it is just a piece of glass and not so rigid without it's wooden door frame, and subject to being broken. What about the metal hardware...the copper hinges which affix the door to the cabinet. They allow the door to open and grant access to the contents. Are they the most important?

No one part can be wholly responsible for the greater sum of all the parts which make up the cabinet. Even the key which has been fashioned solely to fit the lock which holds our cabinet shut has no relevance without a door attached to the cabinet which holds the lock to which our key may turn and grant or deny access to the treasures harbored within. What about the treasures...are they the most important...for they are the whole reason behind building the cabinet in the first place?

It is known by those who study human biology that certain parts of the human brain are responsible for starting the chain of events that produce the chemicals which are responsible for our emotional being. The hypothalamus located deep within our brains produces neuropeptides which are the basic building blocks for proteins which nourish our cells. It is possible that constant bombardment of emotions sets up a BEC-like-state and drives the structure being affected into a feedback loop that becomes biologically addicted to the neuropeptides responsible for particular emotions. For example, if the emotion is brought on by anger then the behavior causes neuropeptides to be produced in the amygdala which are then released throughout the body. If this behavior is continued for long enough it becomes self-sustaining. Addiction occurs and our cells actually begin to crave the same chemicals that cause anger.

This is not to say however that we have no control over our emotions, quite the opposite, we do have the ability to change our addiction to responses that will elicit chemical production of unwanted neuropeptides. Dr Emoto, a noted Japanese biologist and Eastern philosopher, has shown that human emotion has the ability to physically alter the chemical makeup of water. Although little is known about this common substance, it does account for over 90 percent of our bodies. Imagine the possibility of being able to break your chemical dependency on any emotion simply by controlling the chemical substances within your body without the need for anything more than your consciousness.

Life isn't about finding yourself. Life is
About creating yourself.
-George Bernard Shaw

When the soul wishes to experience something
She throws an image of the experience out
Before her and enters into her own image-Meister Eckhart

CHAPTER 3

Hierarchy of Management

Although I currently work in retail, it wasn't always so. I joined the military at an early age, eager to break free of home and parents and to see what the world had to offer. After many years of moving around and experiencing different cultures I settled down and got married. We were young and proclaimed to be in love with each other. After five years the magic ended and divorce replaced our love. I swore off women and concentrated on my life, got a degree in biology and worked various jobs. It was during my college years that I took a course in humanities and had my first taste of that which would re-ignite the fire inside me to seek out the true meaning of life. The course required reading the King James version of the bible and we would discuss each section in great length during class time. I also read much on my own, mostly works from St. Augustine and his own struggle to understand the physical world and the meaning of life.

The first book I ever read that covered the subject of quantum physics was The Quantum Self. The author wrote about the quirkiness of recent discoveries in physics and how they had parallel similarities to human consciousness. The Selfish Gene was my next book which drew in biology and the author made similar relationships rather indirectly as the book was written prior to many of the recent discoveries. I also found Stephen Gould inspirational with all of his layman books written on the subject of evolution and biology. His writing taught me that all that is discovered or proclaimed to be true in biology is not always so and must be reviewed with a critical eye.

I have since read some 200 books ranging from the disciplines of biology, chemistry, mathematics, physics, psychology, theology, philosophy and sociology. Somehow I am drawn to books who central theme revolves around the far-reaching effects quantum physics has had on all of our lives, sometimes without our awareness. But I must say by far the biggest influence on me has been the video "What the Bleep Do We Know?" released in 2005. The resulting cult that has followed the movie swept me up also. It contained everything that I felt inside about the new physics and some of the striking correlations that seem to jump out at all of us from everyday life but we just can't put into words.

Though you lived long ago today you shine bright
Each time I adore you I think of your past and realize
That in your past is revealed your future
And in doing so I have traveled through time and visited places
That will be here tomorrow-today.

The exciting implications of quantum physics give rise to all kinds of possibilities. Take for instance time travel, which is mere speculation and quite irrelevant in quantum terms. It makes much more sense to travel in either direction, past or future to influence events. I guess what I'm trying to postulate is that time travel itself is irrelevant at the level of all that matters. Through our conscious minds we create our own reality and influence all that happens both internally and externally to us. Time travel then becomes merely introspection (memory) when traveling backwards in time. It then follows that travel into the future is only a matter of what we do today that will influence tomorrow. So by having the ability to change our reality, hence our future, through our actions today, we time travel on a regular basis without need for any devices or exceeding the speed of light.

Particles time travel all the time. As elementary particles bump and collide as they go about their business, strange new particles often appear, even if only fleetingly. A basic atom is comprised of a nucleus and electrons orbiting around it. The nucleus contains protons and neutrons. The protons are positively charged and the neutrons are electrically neutral. The positively charged protons are held together by the strong force or exchange of π mesons between them and the neutrons. The electrons, being negatively charged are constantly in motion around the nucleus, their exact location unknown and appearing as a cloud surrounding the nucleus. When particles collide strange things happen. Often what appears at first to be one thing is actually not as it seems. The release of energy is emitted as a photon or quanta of light. What laboratory results reveal when electrons collide under high energies is the release of a photon and a resulting new particle is born sometimes called a quark or even positron. These particles often come from the future or exit into the past. That is to say they time travel.

Why is time travel so alluring to us? Do we need to revisit our past? Should we visit the future? Which direction of travel bears more importance or can produce the most results on events happening now? If we travel into the future do we not also affect the past? And if we visit our past and change things, haven't we in essence just visited the present? Will we be cognizant of the direction from which we came? Will we remember what happened prior to present events, for can we not live outside of the moment? Whether in the past, present or future, it all *is* the same -but the present, and all probabilities become nil. Once we choose one reality or tense all others are lost or conserved. There is only the here and now, to put this in another way---the future has already happened and is always available or at hand, but only influenced by what we choose to happen right now, in the present. Elementary quantum particles often visit from the future, on a regular basis, and depending on events happening here and now, are influenced to maintain the status quo or change slightly or even drastically. How they change and to what degree has a major influence on the shaping of our world. Just imagine particles, like memories, being ever-so-slightly changed in direction and speed as they interact. Every possibility is available to them, as outlined for us by Feynman diagrams. These diagrams contain an infinite amount of possibilities. As one possibility is finally decided upon from the many, then all others are lost (and conserved) with the net result of a similar particle being born that contains *exactly* the same information as it's sister particle. It is therefore acceptable to say that when information is gathered from the particle we have pertinent information as to the future.

We talk about the past and bear memories which help us learn and handle future situations. Without the present there could be no past and certainly no future. To forego any new experience or situation is to neglect oneself the opportunity to time travel. For without memories or prior experience to use as a measuring stick against which to compare, we cannot learn or even see or imagine new situations and experiences. Things simply do not exist for those without a broad level of experiences and information data at their disposal. Learning something new holds no meaning without context and conceptual ambiguity.

You look but do not see
You hear but do not listen
Who is this someone
When you speak of me?

Your forehead with water he touches
Born again Christian
All around others look away
Afraid of what they will see
When they look into your eyes
A quick touch and
Loving embrace before
He withdraws

You look but do not see
You hear but do not listen
Who is this someone
When you speak of me?

Now alone and shivering
Before no one's judgment
He chooses and dies
In vain

An attempt at nothing
Will prevail and those who know
In their hearts
Will grimace

For who was this soul
Lost during his quest
In the perceptions
Of others?

You look but do not see
You hear but do not listen
Who is this someone
When you speak of me?

You cannot know the
Dismal world until you
Have visited this place

That exists in frustration
And the truth so close
At hand
You look but do not see
You hear but do not listen
Who is this someone
When you speak of me?

I seem to have lost track of my original intention for this chapter, that is -how the world of quantum events can be applied to our everyday lives, especially where we spend a great deal of our time -at work. Invariably it is inevitable that those of us who supervise others in a work setting must influence others in such a manner as to "get the job done". It can be challenging, rewarding or downright frustrating to accomplish all of a business' goals without hurting someone's feelings or leaving them feeling left out of the loop. But it doesn't necessarily need be so. By aligning the business to meet the needs of each of it's employees, both the employees and the business can prosper. How can we achieve this?

It has long been a common practice of modern day business to structure it's management in an inverted pyramid, that is with managers at the top and all other employees beneath them. As is the case with many big businesses, for example the military, this may be the ONLY appropriate structure to have. However, even the largest corporations may learn a thing or two from present quantum science. Small businesses with 20 or less employees would benefit the greatest from a management structure that empowers all employees with decision making capability and bearing in mind that it's bottom line is only as strong as the employees which comprise it's essence. After all, any business is nothing more than people and people make or break the business and it's profitability.

Ever notice how a few well motivated employees within a company are the cornerstone upon which all else hangs in the balance?. Now these employees may be managers, but often they are middle or even bottom-of-the-totem-pole people who just seem to be happy all the time, really want to do well and genuinely care about the quality of their work.

So, how do we generate more of these type of people within our business so that all may share in the secret? Certainly we cannot clone them or expect all to have the same enthusiasm or well-being all the time. No, the secret is to be found within each of these particular individuals in their own chemical makeup and attitudes, in the way they conduct their daily lives, and how they deal with the quantum world. What do they possess that others do not? And what can managers learn and apply to ourselves so that we may reap the benefits for our company?

I'll bet if you were to question any one of these particular individuals you would find that even they cannot put into words how or what it is that drives them. Oh sure they may try, maybe explain that that was how they were raised or they do it for self-satisfaction and so on. But these answers do not articulate the how and whys of their successfulness at maintaining a good attitude on a daily basis. Even they do not know the answer. So we will help them out via the quantum world....

First of all I noted that any business is only as strong as it's people. We as managers must realize that they are just that -people, not mindless, feeling-less robots subject to our every whim. Most employees hate nothing worse than not feeling they are part of the TEAM, part of something bigger than themselves. They realize without realizing that the sum of anything's parts is greater than it's whole. This is a priori in quantum systems. They also can work in chaos and may do so better than in an orderly, well-structured program. Those who are creative will suffer the most in suffocating, well-structured management organizations which allow for no lateral movement within it's confines. Out of chaos comes beauty, truth and sometime times highly structured order! This also parallels our quantum world. The bottom line is that we must realize each employees' potential and the environment must be structured around their needs so we may foster their creativity.

Let me back into the next item. For example, there is a small retail store with 10 workers. Two are managers and the rest share varied responsibilities. As a TEAM they strive to achieve the common goal of raising the profitability of the business. One day one of the managers asks one of the workers to do something which that worker knows is against company policy. What is she to do? Do it and risk a scolding or worse yet, termination? Or, should she stand up to the manager and tell him no? Let's first of all give her credit for going through a process of examining all possibilities and their respective outcomes.

So, if she follows through with the request and goes against company policy, one of two things will surely follow, she will be scolded, because the manager has the freedom of pointing his finger at her and saying she did it, relieving him of responsibility or two the manager will be reprimanded. We all know that in reality that more than likely the worker will take the heat and even if only a scolding, she feels the brunt of the incident upon her shoulders and perhaps for some time after it is over.

Perhaps she decides to tell the manager no. What possible outcomes are possible? Well, first of all, how dare she tell the manager no, the audacity of her. Our manager may well up in anger at the act of being challenged and reprimand her on the spot or worse yet take the matter to higher management or even terminate her. Either way, the worker is left scarred and with a bad taste in her mouth for the rest of her days with the company. If this outcome were to be what have we as a manager taught this individual? That the manager gave no alternatives to the worker in itself is probably not a good thing. People must be given freedom to be the creative and quirky individuals they are and not fit into some mould. No one should be judged by personality traits. And certainly we do not want to set examples as leaders that give the impression that our actions are the way we wish others to treat us. And especially, managers must make a conscious effort to realize their own potential, listen with an open mind and take steps to make all conflicts a positive experience for themselves and their employees. A manager must NEVER deny responsibility for his/her actions and if wrong admit it, never cover up or blame others. This just sets the stage for later downfall by workers and presents a facade of acceptable behavior that is NOT acceptable.

> We all know what needs to be done
> Doing it is the hard part…
> -Gen. Norman Schwarzkopf

Secondly, we as managers must strive to talk to individuals in a non-condescending manner. Let's revisit our retail store again for an example of two examples of conversation that carries underlying condescending tones. An employee is going about his business doing his daily routine. The manager comes along and says to the employee that he has not been carrying his weight and must do better before his next review. This is but an example. How does this make the employee feel? And how might the manager handle it differently. Let's assume that it happened in a common area where other employees are present and perhaps a few customers to boot. Now how does the employee feel? The worker may react in anger and end up terminated or worse carry this condescending remark around for a long time, perhaps becoming addicted to and even seeking further ways to elicit similar responses from this same manager.

In our second example the condescending tone is a little more subtle. The same employee is approached and told that statistics show that profitability is down at the particular register that he runs daily, again in front of other employees, who know who the register belongs to. Get the picture? Whether administered directly or subtlety the outcome will be the same. Mostly, managers do this without even realizing their mistake.

Besides the obvious mistake of being condescending and doing so in front of others, managers need to rethink the entire process of reprimand and institute a system of learn by mistake, where feasible, and make it a dialogue where worker input carries as much weight, if not more, as the reprimand itself.

I want to touch again on management structure. It should be that management structures are aligned as such that all know who they are responsible to and for. This is the epitome of a successful business right? I challenge this old-school notion of top down management and rather like to think that the more successful strategy would be to employ not only lateral management, where all employees can make level appropriate decisions for themselves without always seeking a manager. But also having lateral cohesiveness where each employee is doing 2 or 3 other jobs as well as his/her own.

What is it that most managers possess, other than formal education or experience that a frontline worker does not? Information is the answer. Information can be a powerful tool and in the hands of all involved in a business it can genuinely make a business more successful, efficient and ultimately, more profitable. Managers should not be the only recipients of valuable information that matriculates on down from high, this needs to be disseminated to all individuals regardless of their position within a business. And communication carries a similar weight that insures all are on the same page and striving for the common goal whatever it may be for a particular business, efficiency, safety, productivity, profitability etc. Think in terms of particle physics, what bond is beneficial to all parties concerned and extremely strong? Why covalent bonding you reply. Very good! The covalent bond for example which happens between molecules that share a valence electron is a strong relationship and both experience a little of the other and share responsibility for their overall integrity and well-being, perhaps we could learn something from that? The key is being willing to engage the process of change. It helps to remember and be humbled by the fact that our habitual patterns of thought are not useful in helping us get free of those patterns. As Einstein put it, "We cannot solve a problem from the same level from which it was created." I try and visualize harmony with all of my employees by seeing in my mind's eye, all of us seated in a circle, surrounded by rose light, talking heart to heart and accomplishing great work together!

And perhaps most importantly of all, not just for business' or managers, but for all of us as human beings sharing the same rock as it revolves around the sun, we must find ways to change our behaviors on an everyday basis. Stop the neuropeptide addiction. Stop the emotional patterns that get locked into our brains. We can and do change the once thought hard-wiring of our brain. We can change because neurons are inherently flexible and regenerative. So become a better person, manager, Dad, brother, co-worker whatever. Take the first step today, here, NOW! A.H Almaas puts it as such:

> *The moment you become aware of the vicious cycle of the activity of defensiveness, you will see clearly that what you have been rejecting is yourself and that the rejection is useless and unnecessary. Then you will relax and stop. The complete perception of this cycle is the stopping of the wheels. Then the personality is dissolved by clarity. There is clarity because there is no movement in the personality separating it from Being. As you can see, this insight comes only with a great deal of work. It takes a long time to get to the point of seeing the totality of ego activity. To see it experientially and directly rather than from a misidentified or*

transcendent perspective is made possible by a deep exploration of the territory of personality from within. When you see this completely, it is possible for the movement in you that connects you with the rest of society to stop. When it stops, you become pure, clarified personality, soul with no ego structure.

...For the first time, you can perceive the actual substance of the personality without the past.

CHAPTER 4

Creation of the Self

So we vaguely covered some great concepts in prior chapters about the mysteries being uncovered in quantum physics and their relative application to our everyday lives in general. Now, for some of the mechanics of how it all works and how to apply it.

First let me briefly summarize the underlying concepts. Number one being that the quantum world bears striking resemblances to our lives and the way we conceptualize our ideas and thoughts. From a biological standpoint, things we see, think about and store in memory are processed roughly the same as they are in the quantum world. We cannot always say how it is that we do all of this, but every day new discoveries uncover more and more of the mechanics of how the human brain works and where and how information is processed and stored. Striking similarities exist in the human brain to present day computers and their capacity to manipulate information. However none of even the most highly sophisticated computers yet devised even comes close to approximating the neural networks of human biological brains in their ability to process, categorize and store information at the amazing speed at which they do. Furthermore, human brains retain the ability of reasoning and emotion, whereas computers can only apply logic and are not capable of learning from experience. Nor may computers apply experience to future situations. They do have memory, but only in the sense of information stored that may be accessed and applied to a logical set of formal rules and logarithms, unlike human memory which contains the complete experience as discussed in chapter one. That is, a memory contains empirical knowledge. This memory comes complete with information which can elicit sensory perception of smells, sounds and other information gathered and stored during the occurrence of the original event.

So it can be said that computers are best at computation to arrive at some reasonable answer to the question put forth to it, whereas human brains are empirical. They are however, lacking in their ability to later retrieve some information. Tacit knowledge or information which requires the ability to put together a complete package of how we accomplish specific tasks such as the way we drive a car or fly an airplane cannot be specifically translated into logical sequences of events. Flying an airplane only comes after physically flying the plane by the seat of your pants, so to speak. The exact amount of rudder applied is not applicable to all given situations and can only be learned by doing not by being taught. And vice versa teaching it is impossible from the perspective of putting into words the exact way we as pilots move the rudder in response to any given situation. It is possible to draw analogies or use metaphor or euphemism that will approximate the intention of our thought, but it still falls short of the tactile feel of the thought or thing we are holding in our memory.

Just as we made comparison to seeing a thing for the first time, your brain would have no memory or empirical knowledge against which to base sensory input, so certainly it wouldn't be unreasonable to infer that reproducing that tactile feel would naturally be a hard thing to do. Associative memory is the building of neural networks within our brain. They contain the sum of all experiences we have had both consciously and unconsciously in our lives. Approximations show that at any given moment in our lives roughly 400 billion bits of information is bombarding and competing for our attention. At present our awareness only allows us to consciously handle 2000 of these bits. Reality is happening all the time, but our conscious selves can only process a sliver of it at any given time. So, what becomes of all the other stuff? Well, think of reality as a movie playing in front of our eyes. If you realize that your eyes see about like a camera everything that is happening around you at any given second but only capable of holding on to and processing a very small portion, than the film of your brain is subconsciously storing the rest, right? Do we have access to the rest? The brain doesn't know the difference between what it sees and memory. So it stores all that it sees and it follows that we should be able to access it at a later date. It also makes logical sense to apply the concept of reversal of information flow. That is, is the external world more real than the internal world of our brains? What's happening inside should also be available to help create what's happening outside the brain in the external world, at least on a quantum level. The fact that we *may* be influential in creating reality is an interesting possibility, nothing going on outside of the inside of thought. Ideas, concepts and information make up things in the physical world as we see it....

Sadly, we don't know everything about the quantum world and what we do know we understand only vaguely and often times take at face value what we do know to be *theoretically* correct only. Much of the present knowledge exists solely as mathematical concepts and may never be experimentally verified or proven wrong. Some theorists have even begun to think that the expression of the world in mathematical concepts may NOT be the answer to verification, but rather that the math we apply is simply paralleling the results we find in our experimentation. It is further known that all the processes incurred in physics have been the same since the beginning of time and will remain so long into the future. Even universes outside our own must obey the laws of physics as they apply to us here and now.

If the external world is influenced by our observation and our internal thought process does somehow act upon reality how do we account for the *self*? Who and what are we and why are we here? Are *we* part of the universe and reality? Or is life only what we can at present comprehend, some 2000 bits of information? What of the rest? Does it influence also the world which at present we do not understand because we can't? If I look into a mirror and see an image, who is it? Is the image *me*? Or is the reflection *me* and the other just an illusion? Which is *real*?

Symmetry may prove to be one possible answer to what the reflection can tell us about the real world. If you were to look at any- *thing* that is not truly symmetrical in a mirror, you wouldn't see the exact opposite of what is being reflected. That is, if you were looking at the reflection of your left hand, you would see a right hand reflected back, and vice versa. However, if looking at a symmetrical object you would not be able to tell the difference between the *real* object and the reflection. It is also interesting to note here that when looking at a non-symmetrical object in a mirror that being able to tell the difference would be impossible without knowing which *is* real and which is the reflection, so you could compare the differences. And in some cases it is impossible to truly tell which, is the *real* object, and which is the reflection. When looking at particles in a mirror, with minor exceptions, science can tell which, is the real object, and which is the reflection. This is due to the ability to detect angular momentum and velocity, which gives clues to the real object.

Reflected symmetry therefore seems to hold deeper meaning in that it appears to go against our belief in the impossibility of time travel. Take for example, a movie made of an apple falling from a tree. If played in reverse, the apple appears to jump from the ground and defy gravity as it plants itself back on the tree from which it fell. Nothing has been violated as far as physics are concerned. The apple simply traveled back in time and came to final rest from whence it came. You may argue that what really happens is that we are observing an event that has already happened and been recorded on film. But, I would argue that a camera is nothing more than a mirror which reflects back events as they happen. So, viewing the events, whether in forward or reverse produces the same results, the apple moves from some starting point to a final resting point. Potential energy is turned into kinetic energy until reaching either the ground or the tree and energy again equals zero.

Speaking of physics ability to perceive the *real* from the reflection using angular momentum and velocity, it has been detected that every particle that exists in the universe, created in the big bang, has an anti-particle. An anti-particle is the *twin* so to speak of the original, and if we could exploit it, we could gain valuable insight into what the other is doing. Perhaps with the proper technology even utilize the entanglement that exists between the two to transfer information, and since the process would happen at or faster than the speed of light, very interesting possibilities indeed arise from this tantalizing prospect. If one thinks in terms of how time is currently understood, generally in terms of an arrow of time, with time flowing in one direction into the future, then we (in theory) should be able to time travel if we could somehow control the transfer of information from the original particle as it moves both into the past and the future, rejoining at the present. We will discuss this subject next in the following chapter.

CHAPTER 5

The Washing Machine Effect

Human beings already time travel without even giving it a second thought, every second of every day. I remember standing atop a very high cliff in Hawaii with some buddies of mine, looking over the precipice into a very smallish pool of water contemplating the outcome of my survival should I elect to jump. Now, that very process of thinking probably occurred, in terms of time, depending on how you look at it, very rapidly, or very slowly. However, for the sake of my point, we will consider it to have taken place very rapidly. My brain took into consideration many, many variables that could influence the outcome of such an endeavor and made a decision (that probably should have taken a lot longer) in a very short amount of time. How and why? Well, brains are biological entities that can process information rather quickly due to their ability to time travel. Granted, time as we perceive it was passing during the time from which I looked down until the exact moment my feet left the rocks I was standing on, but let's look at how many things happened prior to actually taking that leap of faith….

Again as noted earlier we generally accept time as passing in some forward motion from the now into the future, and science pretty much accepts the smallest theoretical amount of passing -time to be the Planck unit (λ) annotated as 10 to the -43rd power. This is indeed a very small number, actually for visual purposes a decimal point followed by 43 zeros (.0000000000000000……1) while this seems irrelevant, consider the fact that as presently comprehended nothing can happen faster than this time interval, or can it? If something *were* to happen faster than this, say a time interval $(t)<\lambda$, wouldn't travel into the future have occurred? So, let's review.....if t=λ then we are experiencing the present and if t<λ then we are experiencing the future and if t>λ then we are experiencing the past. But, how do we *physically* achieve t<λ ?

Again, back to me standing atop that cliff---as my brain quantumly processed all possible outcomes and scenarios. Actual particles, both of the here-and-now and anti-particles searched my memories, experiences and any associated data that might be relevant to this particular experience. The anti-particle traveled into the past and the here-and-now particle traveled into the future, with the 2 meeting back at the present in t=λ. It was during that processing of information in t<λ that time travel actually took place!

The world also works on this scale all the time, particles come and go from the past and the future as though no time barrier exists whatsoever. Consider electron orbits. As I manipulate the computer to generate pixels on my computer screen, electrons are whizzing in orbit around their respective atoms @ t<λ until I press a key and create their final reality. Could not thought work at the same or *faster* speed as achieved by our orbiting electrons? For example, an orbiting electron is in effect a smearing of possibilities, existing everywhere at once until they 1. Collide with another object and emit a photon, or 2. Are observed or measured and fixed in some location in time and space and become real entities. Sounds an awful lot like time travel to me....

If we could harness this ability to be everywhere at once then stop at some point in our faster-than-light journey we will have time traveled. Of course Einstein's famous theory $E=mc^2$ precludes any possibility of moving a mass the size of our human bodies to very high speeds w/out steadily increasing mass to some infinite amount.

So the whole secret lies in circumventing the speed of light, either achieving it or beating it---many possible thought experiments have come and gone over the years as to just how we might achieve this w/out violating any laws of physics. But by far the most probable is to take advantage of so-called black holes.

For years now, in addition to my never-ending pursuit of explaining how life is possible, I've also been trying to understand how it is that something so simple as a washing machine can contain all the aura and unexplained mystery as contained in the infinite universe. Yes, it is a simple contraption, put the socks in, add some detergent and in a short time they come out clean. Only thing is occasionally one or two *never* come back out of the washing machine. Like any scientist, I have come to accept this as some unwritten and as of yet, unexplainable phenomena that all owners of such devices have come to accept. Where do all those socks go?

A similar phenomenon takes place elsewhere, albeit on a different scale. Black holes are the latest and greatest rage in science now-a-days since their existence first being posited almost a century ago.

Stephen Hawking proposed the existence of these objects in space, perhaps right in our own galaxy. Current hypothesis suggest that many may exist within the entire universe. Black holes are singularities, or rips in the fabric of space-time. So dense and compact and highly unstable that anything that comes near the "mouth" is instantly sucked in to never be seen or heard from again. Actually, gravity is so intense in the interior that anything that does enter cannot possibly escape including light itself.

The upside is that these black holes may allow objects to be transported from one point in time to some point in either the past or future (if they survive the ride). Imagine entering the black hole and actually exiting in the future just seconds before you actually entered in the first place! How weird would that be…not to mention that you may have experienced the time lapse to have been some immense amount of time whereas to an outside observer you appear to be in two places at once, or even as a smeared blob of two possible selves standing at the entrance waiting to go in. (See figure 1.)

The science fiction movie and originally Carl Sagan novel *Contact* was based on this exact sequence of events.

The possibility of ever utilizing such a harsh source of time-travel seems highly unlikely to become a reality. However, science always finds a way, and the possibility of time travel truly looms large on the horizon of future scientific endeavors.

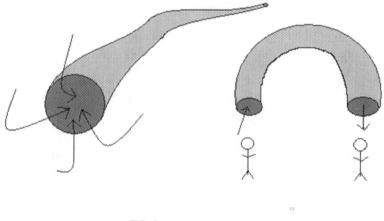

FIG. 1

But, how much do we actually *know* about these hypothetical black holes? Currently science has gone in a number of directions trying to underpin how such a singularity was formed and may exist. Like all good stories we must start at the beginning and see what theory reveals about them.

Since we have not actually seen or been able to study a black hole, we must make some assumptions about what a black hole is and how it would appear if one existed. Most drawings only confuse the matter by making a black hole look like some crazy twister in space, greedily sucking every piece of matter that happens by.

This analogy however, does fit to an extent in that black holes are a singularity where photons cannot escape and time itself stands still. How is it that this could possibly occur?

It just may be possible that our current universe is in itself one grand singularity, at least on the scale of the here-and-now. Roger Penrose has scratched the surface of this theory with his work on the Planck scale of things and how they relate to time and space-time. He believes that most processes that drive the universe exist in states of superposition, constantly competing for discreteness. The Planck scale is a two-dimensional process whereas a small spatial separation corresponds to a longer time and a larger spatial separation to a shorter time. When there is sufficient mass movement between two states under superposition the two space-times differ by 10 to the negative 33rd power/cm.

Bekenstein's-Law stipulates that the area of associated entropy found in the area of the horizon of a black hole is proportional to the information that remains hidden inside it. Another way of thinking about this is to remember the 2nd Law of Thermodynamics which simply states that entropy is only created and cannot be destroyed. If the associated entropy measurement of the horizon is equivalent to the information contained therein we can assume that the horizon is at least an indicator of how much lives inside the black hole. *What* that something is--is currently unknown. The hypothesis of duality, although not the same as the wave-particle duality of quantum theory, also holds tempting implications for usage in this thought experiment. That is that two seemingly different phenomena are just 2 ways of describing the same thing e.g. particles and fields. Charged particles interact not directly, but rather via electric and magnetic fields. It takes a finite amount of time (and thinking along the same lines---*speed)* for information to travel between particles, the information travels via waves in the field. It generally follows a discrete and finite route of the magnetic field to get from one point to another. This is similar to Brownian motion.

Our current world exists on a single plane as it unfolds and spreads around us, with our past trailing behind. The future stretches out in front of us, following the same uncertain superposition of states discussed earlier until some event *happens and makes it a reality.*

Tom Banks put it best when he stated "with an inflating universe we can only see $3\pi/G^2L$ bits of information" where G=Newton's constant L=cosmological constant, also known as the N-bound. So no matter how long we wait, we will never *see* more of the universe than we do now.…..

So, with all that said, how do we see into the black hole? Or at least how do we hypothesize about the information contained within? The energy required to displace even one particle from the gravitational field of another takes $\lambda/2$/gravitational energy=time-scale (T) therefore $T=\lambda/E$. With the impossibility of photons ever escaping the gravitational density found inside a black hole we must think outside the *hole,* so to speak.

It has become increasingly apparent that all the processes involved with our black hole are evolving time frames and relationships trying to achieve a clear choice between a superposition of states. Whether they are achieved via state-vector collapse or the density matrix is dependent upon the relationship happening at a particular moment and what we as observers *bring to the table.* There is no one right description that can describe all these processes, only a series of descriptional relationships between them. Kind of like tacit information being at the front of your brain, but you being unable to translate it into words that will describe a feeling. Even metaphor falls short. If one were to take small "snapshots" as the relationships developed, then therein would lie information pertinent to that one particular moment in time, not the whole story. These "snapshots" however, like a hologram can contain all the information found in the whole, we just can't put it into words.

It may be that the information *appears* to be discrete, but the whole story is continuous and only when the "snapshots" are run in some fashionable time-line sequence that the complete picture evolves. The discreteness of observed moments in time seems to me to indicate, at least in some small way, that quantum duality must exist at all levels of time. It certainly seems rational to think that the relationship carries the most weight and at least allows and leads one to believe that more exists to the parts of the states which one cannot access using either the density matrix or vector-state collapse.

Objective Reduction (OR) and one form or another of string theory and lattices hold at least part of the missing pieces to the puzzle. This is due to their current ability to describe the movement of events and relationships between particles following discrete and finite routes of magnetic fields. The actual choice of changing (minutely) in speed and direction being derived from charged particles not interacting directly, but rather via electric and magnetic fields---the particles traveling via waves in the field, this allows for a finite amount of time and relationally, speed, for information to travel between particles. Two different phenomena now become two ways of describing exactly the same thing, a relationship!

Understanding this relationship will be the key to unlocking the information that lies inside the black hole.

CHAPTER 6

Pursuit of Happiness

The answer lies *outside* of particle physics in the classical sense. The spontaneous breaking of symmetry and related change in mass of one of the members of paired particles *is* affected by a background field. It is this background field that I find most intriguing. The background field exists as a byproduct of human consciousness. And as such is hence influenced by thought, whether directly by meditation or focus, or by indirect means such as experimentation and observation. The two are inexorably linked and describe the same phenomena, experimentally unverifiable only because we are caught and working from inside the framework of the problem itself.

Do we need posit any further, or accept this concept? One of the reasons I personally see this as a truth is that I never disbelieved and actually, read between the lines of what most articles pertaining to this subject elude to. Most particle physicists and theorists indirectly say the same thing, but can't quite take the leap of faith. It's like standing on a windy rooftop pondering in your mind whether if you believe hard enough that you could fly that you just might be able to. It transcends belief alone. If any thought about having *to* believe enters your mind then you are doomed to failure. Most people who think in such ways are often passed off as eccentric and kooky. Even well-educated and famous scientists which on occasion step over the boundary risk losing their reputation. They perhaps are concerned about maintaining the status quo or perhaps being accepted and *allowed* to continue research within academically acceptable boundaries.

We all possess an innate belief as children that things exist that go bump in the night and that we are invincible and capable of doing anything. Heck, I recall the crazy things I did as a kid. My neighbors and parents were taking bets that I wouldn't make it to my 13th birthday. It is only in life that we lose this unconscious ability. We are slowly, seductively desensitized and educated and told how things work. We are unlearned and reprogrammed to tune-in to the status quo. We must all be-on-the-same-page and working-towards-a-common-goal. To an extent this stands true, but letting go of our own subconscious mind over time is in the end-our demise.

You do not even have to accept my words as truth-only that what you know to be true will ultimately set you free. Follow yourself and what your soul screams for you to do and life will never let you down.

This is what particle physics is really telling us. Actually, it is an account of where we have been, where we are going and how to enjoy the trip along the way. The mind knows all, can handle anything that comes it's way and will continually adapt and survive-even on a genetic level. Each and every experience, good or bad, changes us continually. Which experience and how it will change us is totally up to us. Learning how to do this can be hard because of the current environment we live in. Society constantly tells us how to eat, work, play, look and sleep. Think about it, only you should decide how and when and where and why to do things in your life. And paramount of all-technology has gotten darn good at subliminally sending these messages to our subconscious each and every day. Sometimes it's not even accompanied with words, only symbols.

If I were to flash a big yellow M in front of you, you would probably instantly think of whatever it is that attracts you to a certain fast food restaurant. I could bring in many such examples, but that is not my intention here. Advertisers and the media have tapped in to the secret, why can't you and I?

Breaking the addiction of accepting what, how, when, where and why is the 1st step. Addiction to this level of control is hard. Our weak unconscious minds find it easier to accept rather than reject and start over. We as a society on a whole are lazy and don't want to spend any length of time on such matters. However, following your own path means 1st rejection of the status quo-any self-centered behaviors that carry the characteristics of nothing other than egotistical gain need to go! This includes whiter smiles, wearing brand name clothing and having the same car as the Jones' next door. And even extends to mannerisms and body language force-fed to us by the shakers and movers of society.

Change is good, but only if made in the name of peeling back all the layers of built up societal bullshit! Once the addiction of self-fulfillment is overcome may we move on to better understanding ourselves and the nature of human consciousness and behavior.

Happiness is one human addiction that is good for us. Addiction to happiness is the genetic programming which keeps the unconscious mind on the straight and narrow, maintain it's focus and search for truth. "It just feels right" is an old cliché we use which synthesizes this concept into words. You needn't know the biology involved in addiction to happiness, only that once the reversal of ego related behavior is stopped and addiction to happiness is achieved, like a nuclear reaction with unlimited fuel, the process is self-sustaining and will grow in intensity all of it's own accord.

In seeking out happiness we occasionally alter from the path or lose our focus. Sometimes the same pseudo feelings are felt by taking drugs or having sex, but these are cases of over-indulgence. Almost all of us at some point will utilize sex or drugs to enhance feelings of happiness. Many pitfalls lie along the road to happiness, some of which will actually strengthen the process and others which can chip away at the overall effectiveness of the technique. Recognition of which one is encountering will help to ensure positive future experiences (learning from your mistakes).

Now, I am not advocating that anyone release all inhibitions and start doing whatever it is that makes you feel good. My intentions are grounded in scientific relation to the physics of human behavior and the power we can all tap into via our unconscious mind. Bringing our unconscious mind to the surface and recognizing and utilizing it's full potential are two different subjects. We are only focusing on the mind's ability to generate and recognize symbols, metaphors and tacit information so hard to put into words.

One must recognize just as surely as addiction to happiness exists and works, so do a plethora of other addictions to other emotions.

I want to tell you a personal story. I wrote about it and it actually helped me work my way through a bad divorce and almost committing suicide as *I* followed the wrong path.

It mattered not so much that the light hurt his swollen eyes, but that he had been awoken from the most wonderful dream. It was a dream from which he neither could, nor cared to separate from reality. The throbbing in his head was slowly winning the competition and pulling him farther away from the lovely dream, now drifting farther away from his unconscious mind, slipping drearily away, and causing him to focus on the foreground vs. the ambiguous background of his sleepy state. He became aware of sunlight, warm and dappled as it poured in the room. Shadows danced across the walls and the taste of a coppery substance on his lips caused him to wipe his mouth. He winced in pain as he turned his blood-matted head on the pillow, now caked and dry. His other hand touched something cold and metallic. It was smooth and weighty. It's touch flooded his senses with instantaneous remembrance. Something had gone wrong, terribly wrong!

Why did it always happen this way?---and worse yet, why always to him? As he studied the rain drops running pell-mell into larger rivulets eventually gaining momentum and rolling completely off the windshield, he felt sorry for himself---if he could be anywhere but here, now, in this situation. Thoughts were beginning to form verse, verse that would determine his future state of mind and well-being. He hated himself, he hated the rain and mostly he hated her. Would he handle it tactfully, was it possible to handle tactfully? Everything his mind proposed ended in disaster. He had played out each possible scenario, the words, her reactions, and mostly the bitterness, the biting, bitter-sweet remorsefulness of telling the truth. The god-awful truth, the truth that would smite him despite all attempts to remain true to the task---tell the truth, painful and almost sexually stimulating at the same time. Like doing something you shouldn't and getting away with it. Like cheating on a loved one---giving in to the simpler task at hand simply because it requires less energy and will elicit less anger. Did it matter? Would any of it matter, tomorrow? Next week? What about a year from now?

So he began, and as the words mixed with the rain and the warm, moist air, it became easier and easier to give in to the doctrine of self-preservation. Screw her and what she wants and needs...I'm the one hurt here!

And when it was over, the air becomes cooler, perhaps the clouds did subside and maybe the sun shone a little that day, at least in mock pretense of having cleared away the obscurity of lies and deception that had precluded this whole terrible thing. So it went badly, but it could not have gone well. Like the temporary relief felt from vomiting after a great sickness, the relief was only that, temporary, and wave after wave of emotion fought for control of his senses.

A person can just as easily be addicted to anger, jealousy, denial and even depression. One may follow their addiction where they will say and do almost anything to elicit the same feelings to which they are addicted. This is a form of happiness for them, but we are speaking more in terms of happiness which elicit euphoria and feelings of well-being, not just existing to exist, but to some greater end (being at peace with oneself and the world).

I generally proclaim myself atheist and look at most religions with the same criticality as society trying to advocate their beliefs on our unconscious minds. Whether one chooses to believe in a God seems to hold greater implications than just addiction to behaviors which are brought on by societal influence to some extent. To delve into a subject which has been a hotbed since time immemorial is not my intent. Leave it be said that those who choose freely, in principle, to follow the same path of addiction of happiness in their worship, with God as the main focus of their lives, at least parallel the concepts outlined herein.

Even our constitution begins with the words "life, liberty and the pursuit of happiness". It would seem even our forefathers understood the significance of the human unconsciousness and it's homeostatic ability to achieve greatness in all men.

At what point in time did someone or something first realize that it could also be utilized to a different extent? It doesn't require much thought to answer this question. It has and still does exist in all conscious things. If someone who is telekinetic can make an inanimate object move, then there exists a relationship between the person and the object. It doesn't move by some force, rather it moves itself due to the influence of the telekinetic person's mind. The inanimate object must also possess some form of consciousness. So, since life as we now perceive it first existed, it has been evolving and utilizing the ability to influence other conscious objects to it's benefit. We currently call this competition, whether for resources such as space, food, air and water, or even in present day use, attention and money.

If we are to learn from our past mistakes then we must take this lesson seriously and realize that it will probably only worsen. As complex as the world now is in light of what it is *is* what we have made it through manipulation of our unconscious minds, whether directly or otherwise.

Certainly one of the greatest forms of happiness for me, other than finding the perfect woman to marry and having children, was going to college. It required a one hour drive each way to the campus. It was a terrific release of stress and tension. I drove a small car that had standard transmission. I was working as a garage mechanic in those days and I maintained it meticulously.

My daily ritual was to rise early in the pink glow of dawn and drive through the seacoast to Durham, N.H. Like a great symphony the sky brightens and I can hear the high revving four-cylinder engine as it responds to my coaxing. High speed corners, sloshing coffee, downshifting and squealing tires oscillate in rhythm to the blood pounding in my ears. The cacophony rises like a crescendo until I reach the serenity of salt marsh. Giant, white- egrets float above foam filled brackish water. Their great wing beats slow the tempo as the sun follows me through the treetops. There is no place I would rather be than right here, right now with myself and my thoughts.

Becoming is the essence of creativity, intelligence and consciousness, and for an hour, the car and I were one. Happiness is not a destination, but the road we travel to get there and life should be poetry, not prose.

CHAPTER 7

Play the near board!

Many inexperienced hockey players make the mistake of chasing the puck. Rather than utilizing the boards to play the puck or positioning themselves where the puck will finally end up, they haphazardly skate around. Learning to slow down and quickly assess where the game is going makes for successful play. Whoa! You say, *slow* down and *quickly* assess? Yes, the two concepts can be paired together!

Many of us chase the puck. We never play just the basics in life. Those that do are generally the most appreciated people we all know. The ones we engage in conversations because they don't lay a bunch of unwanted advice on us. They live the simpler life. They listen attentively. They genuinely smile. They nurture us and complete us.

With all that we have covered in the last few chapters, I shall now slow things down and play the near board. Some ideas may appear contradictory. This is just like trying to understand quantum physics. Sometimes you just have to let go. Don't try to understand, just get the essence of it. Like trying to explain tacit information, remain stoic and wade through with me.

Know how some days are more taxing on you than others? Ever taken the time to figure out why? Perhaps you chalk it up to bad luck, poor nutrition or that nasty mattress that requires replacing. But, seriously, what is the cause of a bad day. I know for me it usually means an accumulation of things have gotten away from me. Like procrastinating and not utilizing my time wisely, waiting to address the item until the last moment, getting frustrated because something else *always* requires my attention---usually something that I didn't take care of in the first place, or something that I hurried through just to get it done. The old cliché "anything worth doing is worth doing right" suddenly comes to mind…and as much as I hate a cliché, I have used it numerous times. Why? Because it has worth, it doesn't carry the condescending tone of advice and it is basic. It covers the spirit of slowing down and quickly assessing a situation and fixing it correctly at the time of discovery.

Anyways, back to our bad day. In addition to things going undone when needed or getting indiscriminately thrown together, I also focus so much on the nuts and bolts of the task that I never get the bigger picture.

We could all take a lesson from those that hunt. They always seek the highest spot around, or consult a topographical map to see how the terrain looks. It often gives quick clues on where the largest densities of game might be. They can then quickly assess when to be there based on the particular animal's biology, needs and habits.

So, focusing on complexity sometimes leads us astray of the fundamental nature of a problem. Again, slow down and quickly assess that which is embodied in the task by understanding not all the details, but by what the feel of the situation warrants.

After being caught walking with a boy late one night while supposedly walking the dog, our thirteen year old daughter was asked who the boy was. She didn't immediately remember his name or provide much information about him other than he was a nice young man. How did she know this, we inquired, when she didn't even know his name?

"Oh, I just know"…she replied.

It wasn't that she knew little about him, in fact she had known him for many years. To her that information wasn't pertinent to our questioning. To her, it made perfect sense to hang out with someone whom she had already known for many years. She had made a decision based on all the information available to her via her accumulated experience with this particular boy over the years. She had come to know him, his essence and what he stood for, believed in, regardless of whether she remembered his name or not, he was okay in her eyes.

She made a decision grounded in the feel of the situation, not the overwhelming details that we as parents felt existed. I don't use this as an example of justification or claim that either opinion is right or wrong. It is simply an example of tacit information, information that cannot be teased apart without losing the underlying message.

All of us wage war with ourselves. We continually strive to solidify that which we would like to know into that which we know. Unfortunately, we may never know. Science constantly impinges upon our beliefs in what is and isn't possible. With such heavy burdens upon our reality- seeking minds we barely know how to survive in this infinite world.

More and more the decision making process we all use begs to be liberated from that which it has been taught. Within each of us exists unlimited potential, yet we utilize only a fraction of it.

Perhaps we could somehow transcend the traditional thought process of problem solving by being a little less mired down in rationalization and seek resolution rather in the snap decision process that lies on the outskirts of our Freudian slips. After all, nothing happens outside of the inside of thought.

As you may have guessed I play hockey. Both for physical conditioning as well as it's complexity *and* basic structure. Easy. Just get where the puck is going. I have been trying for years. It is a simple and complex game just like life. Just let go. Get to where it is going. Don't get lost along the way. Skate hard and skid in sideways, thoroughly used up and proclaiming "man, what a ride!".

CHAPTER 8

"Can I substitute Fries for chips?"

I am pretty predictable when it comes to meals. If my wife and I go out to eat, I generally order the same thing all the time. However, I don't necessarily feel obligated to have the meal as printed on the menu if it contains items I don't like. Our favorite place to meet for lunch is a little diner on the street above my office. It is the typical greasy-spoon diner comprised of professionals and blue-collar workers and waitresses who know your name and bring you your favorite beverage without you having to ask.

The food can range from great to really bad. I always have a BLT on toasted, homemade wheat with extra mayonnaise and chips instead of fries. But, it wasn't always so...I mean the BLT comes with fries and I had to argue my case that I wouldn't eat the fries and surely shouldn't have to pay for them. So eventually we negotiated for the substitution of chips instead. So now I always get chips with my BLT.

Life can be as simple as a menu. Although you cannot simply order what you want, it does allow for some substitutions. You don't have to have fries if you prefer chips. You certainly have the ability to affect your life each and every day. The quantum world allows for substitutions on a regular basis, if it didn't then all processes and relationships would come to a screeching halt. It is why reality as a world "out there" appears separate from our thought "in here" even though they are one in the same.

Each of us possess' the power to change the reality around us. I am not talking about solid objects like tables and chairs and trees and cars, but rather the processes that all of us as biological entities produce in the course of generating thought. Ever notice how a particular person entering a room will somehow catch the eye of everyone else already in the room. It is as if that particular person is projecting an aura about themselves that is almost visible.

It is this aura that each of us projects that is affected by both ourselves and by others that I am mostly concerned about here. What is this aura and how can we influence it so that each of us may be that person who gets everyone's attention when *we* enter the room? How may we tap into both our own and others to achieve this?

The answer is surprisingly simple. You have already known it. You have countless times promised yourself to do it, but for one reason or another you chose not to follow through. For each ten times you attempted to succeed, there was only one little nagging doubt that tripped you up and you succumbed to failure because you were unable to break the victimization loop of behavior you have slowly become addicted to. It is the same as the marketing schemes of big business, utilizing symbols to brainwash your mind into craving burgers and fries. You have possessed the same skills since you were born. It is natural and predictable. The human brain actually is biologically and genetically programmed to crave certain chemicals which elicit behaviors that we succumb to over and over.

So, don't order straight from the menu. Make up your meal one day at a time. Have chips instead of fries. Don't let society force feed you something you don't want. Don't get addicted to behaviors that you don't like. It is an inversely proportional formula. Getting addicted to a behavior only takes one incident and it gets stronger with each, continual reinforcement.

However, It has been researched and remains fairly consistent that in order to break one bad behavior requires at least twenty tries before an individual may be successful. Are you ready and capable of twenty tries?

Of course you are! You must acknowledge this fact and continually tell yourself that no one can influence your behavior except you and be prepared to fail twenty times before change can take place. Again the relationship is inversely proportional each failure makes the next some number (n) harder than before until enough failures produce a positive result.

Take responsibility for your failures and your successes. As you start to achieve more of these successes it will get easier and eventually you will be the one projecting the aura that everyone notices.

Know what I hate the most?...more than anything else in the whole wide world?...people who pretend to be something they are not...people who look at you, smile in your face, pretend to be your friend...but would just as soon throw you a sack of bricks as you lay floundering in quicksand as they would help you out. Oh...they might put on a façade around others in your presence, all for show...just enough to get by until you are alone with them or when someone's back is turned...then watch out! We have all known or know someone like this. This person also will generally suck all the positive energy right out of you. Surrounding one-self with positive people, people with can-do attitudes, will make your attitude positive also. Negative people are a burden and taxing on our attention span. And as we all know, staying focused and attentive are prerequisites for success in today's busy world.

So be warned, if you encounter one of these energy-sucking vampires, escape as quickly as you can! Don't get seduced into their way of doing things...find your own path and walk fast and steady until their voice can no longer be heard.

I guarantee there will be people who will read this book and they will try to guess what every little phrase, saying, metaphor, analogy and concept is *really* all about. What does he mean by this or that…what influenced such thoughts, where was he at each particular point in his life, career etc.

Well, I am here to clarify so no one will need to guess. There is no great secret to life…let me repeat, there is no great secret to life.

I don't need to wait until I am on my deathbed or become famous to loudly proclaim to you that I have found the secret to anything let alone the secret to life. Life is about living…living and the relationships that will certainly happen as you go about living. Learn everything you can along the way before one story ends and you have to start all over again…

I cannot complete this chapter, (or this book), without writing about my current state of mind. I mean how I feel now, here, today as I write and pour forth my emotions, thoughts and yes; frustrations. Frustrations that stem mainly from within myself, but are also fueled by society as a whole and the way we choose to view ourselves and each other. I can honestly say (it's almost the only honest thought I have these days) that I do sympathize with anyone who is campaigning for a *cause*, by using this obscure word I mean, anything that really gets them HOT under the collar. Now, I am not justifying behaviors, or anything else that may come about from someone's pursuit of a *cause*, but just sympathizing with the harsh realities that come along with banging headlong into an uncomforting world that paints a concept of what is morally right and wrong simply by writing them down in words and expecting everything else to fall into place. No acceptance is given for anything else other than what we say is right or wrong! How brain-dead can we be…who are we to pass judgment? Who do we think we are?

I have to believe that even 100 years ago life was simpler than today. The complexities of navigating life were surely less strenuous when they didn't include high mortgages and outrageously priced college tuitions. One could simply cut down more trees and supply himself with both fuel to heat his home as well as clear more land to grow more crops. What option have we left ourselves today when our high salaried position is no longer sufficient to make the mortgage and all the other bills? Where do we turn when our sons and daughters seek more comfort from the internet than they do from parents, relatives, and their friends? What shall we do when we no longer can face ourselves in the morning mirror? All I can say is please stay within your stereotype, please, if you are a loser, play the part of a loser. If you are a rich, arrogant, S.O.B. than be a rich, arrogant, S.O.B. Don't pretend to be someone or something that you are not…

Money and for a lack of proper words, influence, are two facades that remain elusive in the Upper Valley where I live, work and play. You are either a Doctor, studying to be a Doctor or a business owner or you struggle with a meager salary or hourly rate that requires both spouses to work full-time jobs to make ends meet. You are so tired at the end of a typical work week that you really haven't the stamina you expend to argue with your spouse, whom you used to really love before getting into this jamb, about not having enough money to make ends meet! It's a vicious cycle. You can't attend town meetings pertinent to the latest Wal-Mart applying for a building permit next door, because you have to work. You have to work because you can't make ends meet…before you know it you're so poor you can't afford to pay attention!

Whew! A lot said back there…but it helps one to clear the mind and continue with the argument. One thing I remember doing earlier in my childhood, oh, around the time I was maybe ten years old, was having chronic nightmares. Usually they consisted of being chased by monsters and often bears. These dreams about bears continued well into my adulthood and really began to bother me. Often I would be running and just jump up and begin flying and fly right out harm's way. But, sometimes I wouldn't possess the power to do so. I was aware that I was dreaming and seemed quite capable of manipulating my dreams. So eventually I tried a little experiment. Before going to sleep at night I would envision a jukebox in front of me. It contained not songs, but a selection of dreams. I would place a coin into the jukebox and select a dream to have that night. It worked very well. I could even stop a dream in the middle and select a different dream if the first didn't work out. Life itself appears to me as the same principle, one has simply to wish something into being real. I often create my day before I ever shut off the alarm clock and head out to work. I know exactly how everything will go, where the troubles lie ahead and even the day that I will die.

I am no longer afraid of the dark, bears chasing me or the unknown because now, all is known, because I create it just the way I like it, chips… no fries.

CHAPTER 9

Quantum Relationships

Right here. Right now. How do I feel? I almost want to refuse to answer that question. I have spent the last couple of hours talking to the woman whom I fell in love with and married. Actually we were impersonally texting each other. And quite actually the texting only lasted a very few minutes. Probably only 1 minute all told if you didn't count the gap in between waiting and then reading and then texting back. It is the safe way to "talk" without having to deal with tonal voice quality, or perceived Gottman-inuendos. She is in Boston, Natick, where she has been all day. Refusing to be honest and share where she is and what she is doing. The worst of all situations for anyone, lest a husband who has worked all day, come home and picked up the house, walked the dog, barely had time to eat, then deal with an uncooperative spouse who refuses to be honest. Perhaps she has known for awhile that she would be taking this trip, perhaps not. Either way is safe. Not sharing is all the worst for it leaves the mind room to fill in the gaps. Our marriage has been dying and now that she has decided to fill in her own gaps and leave mine blank, I feel hostile. But that approach has already proven futile. Being "friends" has not worked. Marriage counseling is just another excuse to elicit old feelings that obscure the truth of the current matter. I want to make it work and have been trying to change, but she due to too many years of neglect, or just plain giving up has been preventing anything positive from happening. Now it can be argued anyway you want. Everything is open to interpretation. I am the master of interpretation. However, she is stoic and giving nothing. It is like a weekend barbeque where everyone brings something to the feast except one who only drops in to eat and then leaves. Her attitude has changed, her demeanor more serious, taking on the qualities she always claims to have disliked in other people. Funny how that works---her ability to not judge people was one quality I always adored in her---her smile, her "I always have time for you" attitude, no matter the workload or stresses she was currently under. All this is slowly and seductively stripped away. It is as though we have reversed roles. I am now the talkative, caring one and she, the; "I gotta' go…" one. How could this be?

Many such relationships other than those between bickering spouses exist. Quantum physics allows for all kinds of weirdness, although weirdness is closer to the norm than it implies. This is most likely because there is no scale yet understood or capable of wrapping our heads around. One could spend years in counseling or mitigation over the subject just like spousal relationships, but the solution may never be attained. How does this make you feel? I know how it makes me feel, I am experiencing both the issues and feel like I did when taking my first Finite Math course in college. Finite to me implies that something is attainable---*possible*. Never give up. I have always remained hopeful.

Infinity on the other hand, well that just can't be. There can't be no end to something! Absurd! Impossible! Just like my free-spirited, role reversing wife, it can and is so. Everything is possible (until it becomes not). Sounds all too simple, alluring, yet complicated. The premises that are underlying in quantum events demand a second look. They are not what they appear to be. Give them space. Back off and give it time.

Ever stand on the downwind side of a campfire? Smoke gets in your eyes. It doesn't care that you are enjoying your scotch. It just is. Some things are like this and our attempts to scrutinize only make the obscurity worse. For those of us always on this edge is where we function best. Chaos, erratic behavior, it all adds fuel to the fire. Makes us keep chasing the elusive answer, always there, right on the tip of your tongue. Like a familiar face sharing some space on a crowded subway in Manhattan while visiting your daughter, you nod your head, smile and say "how you been?", hoping that the face will divulge who he is so you won't feel terrible because he remembered you, but you can't remember his name.

Like the human psyche going through a mid-life crisis, where the divergence of two opposing behaviors causes one to have a nervous breakdown, quantum physics seeks to lie on the outskirts of our imagination. The outskirts are it's perturbation point as referred to by physicists. The place where we barely are cognizant of it's existence. Like our unconscious mind, small glimpses appear fleetingly that titillate our conscious mind. They may appear in a Jungian dream. They may appear as synchronicities, or de-ja vu. There is something guttural in human nature about new discovery. It has been inside all of us, a sleeping giant awakened occasionally. It teases us, gives us a view that is obscured like flying IFR on a socked in day. The instruments can only tell you so much and you are forced to their attention, giving in to stolen glances outside the cockpit window at the elusive ground below. It is a hair-raising experience, but somehow thrilling.

I watched a television show the other night which was taking advantage of some latest breakthrough in quantum entanglement to encrypt information over the internet, stronger and more reliable than a firewall. Just the mere act of a hacker looking at it changes the information, renders it useless. Incredible, yet true, I remember the young post doc who was first to discover it's potential in just such a scenario. He hadn't refined anything, but knew that he was on to something. Unfortunately the technology is so complicated that it is unusable beyond distances of fiber optic cable much longer than fifty miles. However, it won't be long before we are employing it to it's full potential. So, now would be the time to invest heavily in R&D companies who are financing further developments. The 19th century was an era of intergalactic exploration, the twentieth century one of physics and our current endeavors are focused on information technology to contain and enhance the large volume of technology that looms on the cusp of tomorrow. In other words, we know about and have dabbled in many things, but need to keep pace with and contain this growing technology so that it stays linear and progresses without getting out of hand. Every day we silently wake and live out our lives without really giving a second thought to all that is being researched, developed and employed as we sit lazily at our computer workstations or engulfed in the latest energy crunch or political campaign. Oh, we may be blissfully aware and numb to certain things we hear or see or read in Scientific American at the dentist office, but think about it, how much do we really know? As noted in earlier chapters, the human brain automatically seeks new information, or put succinctly, information that it has been genetically predisposed to. Finding the key hole to unlock it, at least to me seems to be the necessary ingredient.

I firmly believe that all the information contained in the universe is available in all of our minds. We are, and contain all since the beginning. Releasing that information is what we as a race strive all our lives to do without realizing it. Each and every one of us has the potential to "discover" some great piece of the puzzle. When a number of us do this together, the puzzle will begin to take on color, shape and the obscurity will begin to clarify and the picture *will* start to take shape, a living shape all it's own. When that day happens I will be there laughing at myself, because I trust the picture will be of me…staring at myself in some weird quantum mirror.

BIBLIOGRAPHY

Ford, Kenneth
The Quantum World
Harvard University Press 2004

Magueijo, Joao
Faster than the Speed of Light
Penguin Books 2003

Lederman, Leon
The God Particle
Houghton-Miflin Co 1993

Bruce, Colin
Schrodinger's Rabbits
Joseph Henry Press 2004

Lederman, Leon
Symmetry and the beautiful universe
Prometheus Books 2004

Zohar, Dana
The Quantum Self

Smolin, Lee
Quantum Gravity
Basic Books 2001

Randles, Jerry
Breaking the Time Barrier
Simon & Schuster 2005

Mccarthy, Wil
Hacking Matter
Basic Books 2003

Gladwell, Malcolm
Blink
Little, Brown & Co 2005

Talbot, Michael
Mysticism & the New Physics
Arkana Penguin Books 1993

Laughlin, Robert B.
A Different Universe
Basic Books 2005

The Atlas of Life on Earth
Border's Press 2004

Talbot, Michael
The Holographic Universe
Harper-Perennial 1991

Peat, F. David
Synchronicity, The Bridge Between
Matter and Mind
Bantam New Age Books 1987

Steven J. Bingel

Fred Alan Wolf, Ph.D.
Mind Into Matter
Moment Point Press 2001

Penrose, Roger
The Large, the small and the
Human Mind
Canto Press Cambridge University 2000

Walker, Evan Harris
The Physics of consciousness
Perseus books 2000

Fred Alan Wolf Ph.D.
The Spiritual Universe
Moment Point Press Inc 1999

Krauss, Lawrence
ATOM
Little, Brown & Co 2002

Kindersley, Dorling
Ultimate Visual Dictionary
Of Science
DK Press 1998

Lide, David
Handbook of chemistry & physics 85th Ed
2004-2005 CRC Press

Black, Jacquelyn G
Microbiology, Principles & Explorations 6th Ed
John Willey & Sons Inc 2005

Dawkins, Richard
The Selfish Gene
Oxford University Press 1976

Simon Barron-Cohen
The Essential Difference
Basic Books 2003

Matthieu Ricard & Trinh Xuan Thuan
The Quantum & the lotus
Three Rivers Press 2001

Schrodinger, Erwin
What is Life?
Cambridge Publishing 1944

Susskind, Leonard & Lindesay, James
Black Holes, Information and the String
Theory Revolution
World Scientific Publishing 2005

Davies, Paul
The Mind of God
Simon & Schuster 1992

Dudley, Glen
Infinity and The Brain

The Author currently resides in Norwich, V.T. with his wife Maureen. They have 7 children and four grandchildren. Steven attended the University of New Hampshire after separating from the United States Air Force in 1990. After working for the U.S. Fish and Wildlife Service he moved to the Upper Valley. He has been employed at West Lebanon Feed & Supply for 21 years and plans an early retirement in 2019.

Steven enjoys hunting, fishing, playing ice hockey and playing guitar. In his spare time he writes. This is his second book. The first was Mudville published in 2014. Although not a classically trained physicist, he enjoys reading about quantum physics and has his own views on how the mysteries of this subject can be understood in analogies and everyday life experiences.